THE INCREDIBLE BOSTON RED SOX TRIVIA BOOK

THE INCREDIBLE BOSTON RED SOX TRIVIA BOOK

300 QUESTIONS FOR THE SUPER-FAN

BILL NOWLIN

Sports Publishing books may be purchased in bulk at special discounts for sales promotion, corporate gifts, fund-raising, or educational purposes. Special editions can also be created to specifications. For details, contact the Special Sales Department, Sports Publishing, 307 Fifth Avenue, 4th Floor, New York, NY 10016 or sportspubbooks@skyhorsepublishing.com.

Sports Publishing® is a registered trademark of Skyhorse Publishing, Inc.®, a Delaware corporation.

Visit our website at www.sportspubbooks.com.

10 9 8 7 6 5 4 3 2 1

Library of Congress Cataloging-in-Publication Data is available on file.

Cover design by David Ter-Avaneysan
Cover photos credit: Getty Images

Print ISBN: 978-1-68358-529-9
Ebook ISBN: 978-1-68358-530-5

Printed in the United States of America

Contents

Introduction

What, another book of baseball trivia? Yes! I've got a couple of dozen such books around the house.

I've even written some of them myself—depending on your definition of what is trivia (see, for instance, *Red Sox By the Numbers*, written with Matt Silverman and published by Skyhorse back in 2010, or *So You Think You're a Boston Red Sox Fan?* which was published in 2017 by Sports Publishing). If you love a team (even a team that never won a World Series in your lifetime until you were more than half a century old), there are many different ways to look at the unfolding story of the team and its players. You never know what you might come across.

During the 2025 season, I realized that two of the twenty-five players on Red Sox active roster had the same birthday, and then learned that it was also the birthday of a child of the team's head of Media Relations.

In the same season, I was fortunate to be present at Fenway, on June 30, to see Wilyer Abreu hit both an inside-the-park home run and a grand slam *in the same game*. The last player to do that was Roger Maris in 1958. The only other Red Sox player to do it was Jim Tabor, on July 4, 1939. You just never know what you might see. I once saw the Red Sox hit into two triple plays in the same game—and they still won! I even saw them win the final game of the World Series at Fenway Park in 2013, the first time they had done that since 1918.

Some of the greatest moments in Red Sox history are ones none of us have ever seen—and are not even available on YouTube (any of Cy Young's games, for example). But they're in newspapers, history books, and have been written up by SABR members and other baseball aficionados.

I was born into Red Sox nation, my father having worked as a hot dog vendor at Fenway in 1937 and 1938—though he wasn't enough of an historian to be able to tell me the first game he ever took me to. There really weren't all that many he took me to; he had to work. By the time I was twelve, I was going to at least a dozen games a year on my own. Back then, a bleacher seat cost 50 cents.

I haven't gone far in life. I live just under four miles from Fenway, which is just 4.1 miles from where I was born. Fenway is kind of a home away from home. Thanks to all who were part of the Save Fenway Park! movement about twenty-five years ago, and thanks to current ownership for, in fact, saving the ballpark.

Most diehard fans—and even plenty of casual ones—enjoy baseball trivia. I enjoyed digging in deeply and working up the 300 items in this volume. I'm confident that readers will find a few surprises here, and hopefully some enjoyment. They are presented with Red Sox fans in mind, offered in a number of categories as a way of offering different opportunities for differing perspectives. Offense and defense, rookies and veterans, ballparks and championships, even locales. As noted in one question: there are only eight of the fifty United States in which the Red Sox have yet to play. Speaking as someone who has seen them play in five different countries, I'd like to see them visit those remaining states.

I'm hopeful readers will find some new and fascinating items here. I did, while working on the book. Try some of them out on your friends. Enjoy reading the book. It was a pleasure working on it.

Bill Nowlin

BATTING

1. Which Red Sox player had the best single-season batting average?
   Answer on page 7.

2. Which Red Sox player holds the career mark for the best on-base percentage?
   Answer on page 7.

3. Which rookie holds the record for the most walks their first year?
   Answer on page 7.

4. The number 406 crops up again. Who holds the record for the most total bases in one season?
   Answer on page 7.

5. Which player set the record for the most doubles in one season?
   Answer on page 7.

6. Which player holds the record for most base hits in one season?
   Answer on page 7.

7. Which player has the team record for the most doubles in his career?
   Answer on page 7.

8. Which player holds the team records for most hits, most RBIs, most runs scored, most extra-base hits, and most total bases?
Answer on page 7.

9. Hitting for the cycle—it's been done 23 times. Who's the only team player to do it twice during regular-season games?
Answer on page 7.

10. There was one Red Sox player who hit for the cycle in a post-season game, the only major leaguer to ever do so. He'd already done it once in the regular season but then did so in the post-season—against the Yankees, no less. Who was he?
Answer on page 8.

11. Two Red Sox players have won the Triple Crown (leading the league in batting average, home runs, and runs batted in—all in the same year). Who were they?
Answer on page 8.

12. Driving in 100 runs in a season is a true milestone. Which Red Sox player had the most 100-RBI seasons?
Answer on page 8.

13. Who once drove in one or more runs in 10 consecutive Red Sox games?
Answer on page 8.

14. Who once drove in 10 runs, all in one game?
Answer on page 8.

15. Who holds the longest hitting streak in Red Sox record history?
Answer on page 8.

16. Which Red Sox player holds the major-league record for the most consecutive games reaching base safely? Call that CGOBS.
Answer on page 8.

17. What Red Sox player knocked out more than 200 hits each of his first three years in the majors?
Answer on page 8.

18. In terms of team offense, what is the largest number of runs the Red Sox ever scored in just one inning?
Answer on page 8.

19. Which Red Sox player has the most walk-off RBIs?
Answer on page 9.

20. The Red Sox played 163 games in 1985 (there was one tie). Wade Boggs played in all but two of them. In how many games was he unable to get on base?
Answer on page 9.

21. In 2018, three Red Sox players each scored more than 100 runs. Can you name all three?
Answer on page 9.

22. The Silver Slugger Award has only been given since 1980. Which Red Sox player won it the most times?
Answer on page 9.

23. Heading into his sixth season in big-league ball, what trajectory was Nomar Garciaparra unable to maintain?
Answer on page 9.

24. In terms of driving in runs while pinch-hitting, who holds the major-league record for the most RBIs in one season?
Answer on page 9.

25. Who holds the American League's best season batting average for a pinch-hitter, with a minimum of 10 at-bats?
Answer on page 9.

26. Which Red Sox batter once had two pinch-hits in the same inning? He also scored twice in that inning.
Answer on page 9.

27. In 1969, Rico Petrocelli set a team shortstop record that has held for 56 years. What was it?
Answer on page 9.

28. Who holds the Red Sox record for most RBIs in a single season?
Answer on page 9.

29. Ted Williams won six batting titles. He just missed a seventh in one other year—the mathematically closest second-place finish ever. Who edged him out?
Answer on page 10.

30. Wade Boggs hit .400 over the course of 162 games. True or false?
Answer on page 10.

31. Which Red Sox batter reached base safely in 16 consecutive plate appearances?
Answer on page 10.

32. Who was the last American Leaguer to rack up more than 400 total bases in a season?
Answer on page 10.

33. Twice, Red Sox batters were 6-for-6 in a game. Who were the two batters?
Answer on page 10.

34. These two batters both drove in one or more runs in 12 consecutive games. Who were they?
Answer on page 10.

35. This Red Sox player once assembled 12 base hits in 12 consecutive at-bats. Who was he?
Answer on page 10.

36. What non-pitcher on the Red Sox got an RBI in his first game, without an at-bat, then waited five years for his second one?
Answer on page 10.

37. There are 44 Red Sox players who had only one career base hit, ever, through 2025—despite having as many as (in one case) 22 plate appearances. Can you name them all?
Answer on page 10.

38. This New England–born Red Sox batter played in 13 games for the Red Sox, with 23 plate appearances, but never got a hit. He walked four times and scored a run, but never got a hit. Who was he?
Answer on page 11.

39. Can you identify the game in which there were 19 times the Red Sox got a runner into scoring position, but couldn't get him home?
Answer on page 11.

40. Making a good first impression, what Red Sox player pinch-hit and both tied and then won that game in his first two at-bats for Boston?
Answer on page 11.

BATTING

ANSWERS

1. Ted Williams, .406 in 1941. Williams batted left-handed. The best average for a right-handed batter was .372, by Nomar Garciaparra in the year 2000.

2. Perhaps the most remarkable accomplishment of all—Ted Williams's lifetime mark was .482. In other words, 48.2 percent of the times he came to bat, Ted Williams got on base.

3. With solid plate discipline from the start, it was Ted Williams who walked 107 times in 1939.

4. Jim Rice, with 406 total bases in his MVP year, 1978. He led the majors with 46 homers and with 15 triples, and with 213 base hits in all.

5. Earl Webb, with 67 doubles in 1931.

6. In 1985, Wade Boggs had 240 base hits—and a majors-leading .368 batting average.

7. Carl Yastrzemski doubled 646 times.

8. Yaz. Hits = 3,419 (765 more than Ted Williams), RBIs = 1844 (3 more than Ted), runs scored = 1,816, extra-base hits = 1,157, and total bases (5,539).

9. Bobby Doerr—on May 17, 1944, and May 13, 1947.

10. The "Brock Star"—Brock Holt. On June 16, 2015, he hit for a cycle against Atlanta and then in Game Three of the 2018 American League Division Series (October 8, 2018) he did so in New York.

11. Ted and Yaz. Ted Williams—twice, in 1942 and again in 1947. Carl Yastrzemski, in 1967. In between the two Ted Williams stints were three seasons in which he was in military service during World War II. One wonders how he might have filled in those years had he been able to continue to play ball.

12. David Ortiz did it 10 times. They accounted for most of his 1,530 Red Sox RBIs.

13. On September 14, 2002, Manny Ramírez hit two solo home runs to help beat the Orioles. For every one of the next nine games, he drove in one or more runs, for an uninterrupted 10-game stretch. The team won eight of those 10 games.

14. Four different Red Sox players have accomplished this feat: Rudy York (July 27, 1946), Norm Zauchin (May 27, 1955), Fred Lynn (June 18, 1975), and Nomar Garciaparra (May 10, 1999). The Red Sox won all those games—13–6, 16–0, 15–1, and 12–4.

15. Joe DiMaggio's younger brother, Dom, who hit safely in 34 consecutive games in 1949.

16. In 1949, there was a stretch in which Ted Williams reached base in 84 consecutive games from July 1 through September 28.

17. Johnny Pesky led the league each year, with 205 hits in 1942, and then came back after three years in wartime military service to hit 208 in 1946, and 207 in 1947.

18. In the bottom of the seventh inning on June 18, building on a 5–2 lead over visiting Detroit, the Red Sox scored 17 runs. They won the game (not a surprise, given the inning), 23–3. There were 14 hits in the inning but only one home run. George Kell made two of the three outs, and left the bases loaded with his inning-ending second fly-ball out.

Gene Stephens had a record three base hits in the one inning. Remarkably just the day before, Boston had beaten the Tigers 17–1.

19. David Ortiz has 17 walk-offs to his credit. Yaz is second with 14.

20. Just 11 of them.

21. They were Andrew Benintendi (103), J. D. Martinez (111), and—leading all major leaguers that year—Mookie Betts (129).

22. David Ortiz (seven times). Manny Ramírez won the award nine times and Wade Boggs eight times, but Manny's first three were as a member of the Cleveland Indians, while Boggs's last two were with the Yankees.

23. Increasing his batting average every year—starting in 1996 (just 24 games that first season), through the year 2000, his batting averages were: .241, .306, .323, .357, and .372. Considering the first four full seasons, with a mathematical average increase of 22 points per season, his mark in 2001 could have been .394—but he missed the first 17 weeks of the season due to surgery.

24. Joe Cronin, with 25 in 1943. He is tied by Jerry Lynch of the Cincinnati Reds (1961) and Rusty Staub of the New York Mets (1983).

25. In 1983, Rick Miller compiled a .45714 average as a pinch-hitter. He hit .286 overall. Ed Kranepool of the 1974 Mets hit a major league–leading .48571 as a pinch-hitter.

26. Russ Nixon, on May 4, 1962. In the bottom of the fifth, the White Sox led, 4–0. Nixon pinch-hit for starter Mike Fornieles and singled off Ray Herbert. Every one of the next eight batters reached base, too, bringing up Nixon again. Eddie Fisher was Chicago's fourth pitcher of the inning. Nixon singled again, driving in two. By the time the inning was over, Boston had 12 runs and went on to win, 13–6.

27. He hit 40 home runs in the one season.

28. Jimmie Foxx, with 175 RBIs in 1938. The most driven in by a left-handed batter was Ted Williams's 159 in 1949.

29. In 1949, Williams hit .3427561 while George Kell hit .3429118. Both rounded off to .343, but Kell hit .0001557 above Williams.

30. True—but not all 162 games were in the same season. The first game in the stretch was on June 13, 1985, and the 162nd game was on June 8, 1986.

31. It was thirty-nine-year-old Ted Williams. From his pinch-hit homer on September 17, 1957, through the September 23 game in which he singled, walked three times, and finally was hit by a pitch, he reached base 16 consecutive times. Four of the 16 were home runs.

32. It was Jim Rice of the Red Sox in 1978, with a total of 406. He led the majors in hits (213). triples (15), homers (46), and—for that matter—RBIs, with 139. Unsurprisingly, he was the AL MVP.

33. Jimmy Piersall on June 10, 1953, and Nomar Garciaparra on June 21, 2003. Three days later, on June 24, Nomar went 5-for-5.

34. Joe Cronin (June 27, 1939, through the first game of the July 9 doubleheader—twice with his only RBI coming on a sacrifice fly) and Ted Williams (August 31, 1942, through the first game of the August 13 doubleheader). Ted's total was all on base hits, producing 18 RBIs over those 12 games.

35. Mike "Pinky" Higgins, starting with four hits in his last four at-bats of a doubleheader in Chicago on June 19, 1938. The next day, the Red Sox played another doubleheader, this time in Detroit. Higgins was 4-for-4 in the first game and 4-for-4 in the second game. There were a couple of walks in there, too, but he was 12-for-12 in successive at-bats.

36. Jim Pagliaroni drove in a run on a sacrifice fly on August 13, 1955. His next RBI came on August 4, 1960—and drove in the go-ahead run in a 3–1 win over KC.

37. Yes, you could—if you looked them up. Sparing readers the chore, we will note that Hal Kolstad stands out. A right-handed pitcher, he worked in 1962 and 1963 and was 1-for-22, for a career batting average of .053. He struck out 10 times. The hit was a single to left on June 28, 1962, in a game that the Angels won 19–7. Only 3,903 in attendance can legitimately claim to have seen it. As this book goes to press, there is still hope for one player on the team in 2026—Garrett Whitlock.

38. Mickey Gasper, in 2024.

39. On April 24, 2004, the Red Sox beat the Yankees in 12 innings, 3–2, at Yankee Stadium. Every one of their three runs scored on a sacrifice fly.

40. Darnell McDonald, on April 20, 2010. Pinch-hitting in the bottom of the eighth, his two-run homer tied the game against the Rangers, 6–6. He came to bat again in the bottom of the ninth, with two outs and the bases loaded, and singled in Kevin Youkilis to win the game, 7–6.

BASERUNNING

1. Who holds the team record for most stolen bases in one season?
   Answer on page 15.

2. Who holds the team record for most stolen bases over the course of their career?
   Answer on page 15.

3. Who holds the American League record for most consecutive stolen bases before getting caught?
   Answer on page 15.

4. Getting runners on base is one thing; scoring them is another. What is the largest number of runners the Red Sox left on base during a game on which they were shut out?
   Answer on page 15.

5. Which Red Sox player drew the most walks—one after the other—in a given game?
   Answer on page 15.

6. Who holds the record for the most stolen bases in a single game?
   Answer on page 15.

7. What is the team record for stolen bases in one game?
   Answer on page 16.

8. The least theft-oriented team? Which year did the team leader only steal five bases?
Answer on page 16.

9. Can you name the pinch-runner who came into a game and hit a grand slam that inning?
Answer on page 16.

10. Who stole more bases than any other Red Sox player?
Answer on page 16.

BASERUNNING

ANSWERS

1. Jacoby Ellsbury, who stole 70 bases in 2009. You've got to get on base to be able to steal one. Ellsbury hit .301 that season and walked 49 times.

2. Harry Hooper, who stole exactly 300 while with the Red Sox.

3. Trevor Story, 31 consecutive steals, starting on Opening Day on March 27, 2025, until he finally got caught—just once all year—on September 17.

4. Fourteen! The Red Sox placed first in the AL East in 1988, but on May 16, they had seven base hits, and the visiting Oakland Athletics treated them to seven walks. Starter Storm Davis threw three wild pitches. They loaded the bases in the second and the fourth, and got a runner to third base in the fifth and to second in the eighth, but they couldn't bring even one man home.

5. Jimmie Foxx walked six times in six plate appearances on June 16, 1938—one intentional. He scored two times. Boston beat the St. Louis Browns at Sportsman's Park, 12–8.

6. Jacoby Ellsbury, who stole five bases on May 30, 2013, against the Phillies. The Red Sox won, 9–2, but not one of Ellsbury's steals was involved in any of the scoring.

7. The record is nine, set by the Red Sox against the Yankees on June 16, 2024. David Hamilton stole four of the nine and later scored three of the four runs. Boston beat the Yankees, 9–3.

8. In 1960, on a team that stole a combined 34 bases, Pete Runnels and Gene Stephens each swiped five, tops of the team.

9. If you said Gene Stephens, you are right. On July13, 1959, after Ted Williams singled in a run in the bottom of the sixth to make it Red Sox 5, Yankees 2, he was removed for a pinch-runner. Red Sox batters kept hitting and took a 9–2 lead. His spot in the order came up again and it was Stephens who hit a grand slam off Jim Bronstad to make it 13–2, which stood as the final score.

10. Harry Hooper, who stole exactly 300 bases in his 12 seasons with the Red Sox.

HOME RUNS

1. Who had the most extra-inning home runs for the Red Sox?
   Answer on page 21.

2. Which player holds the team record for most career grand slams?
   Answer on page 21.

3. Which player holds the team record for the most grand slams in one season?
   Answer on page 21.

4. In both 1915 and 1916, Babe Ruth led the Red Sox in home runs. How many did he hit each year?
   Answer on page 21.

5. Ted Williams once pitched in a game, but one thing he never did was bat right-handed. The Sox did have a switch-hitter who once hit a grand slam batting right-handed, then hit another grand slam in the very same game, batting left-handed. Who was he?
   Answer on page 21.

6. Which Red Sox player holds the team record for most homers in one season?
   Answer on page 21.

7. Who leads the Red Sox in multi-homer games during a season?
   Answer on page 21.

8. Of those games, how many times did the second homer make the difference and give the Red Sox a win?
Answer on page 21.

9. Take a guess as to how many game-ending grand slams Red Sox players have hit—more than 10?
Answer on page 21.

10. Which two Red Sox players hit grand slams as their first big-league base hits?
Answer on page 22.

11. Which Red Sox player hit a walk-off grand slam in his first game with the team?
Answer on page 22.

12. Which Red Sox player is the only one with two walk-off grand slams?
Answer on page 22.

13. Who is the only Red Sox player to hit a walk-off grand slam against the New York Yankees?
Answer on page 22.

14. Whose 16th inning walk-off grand slam finally brought the game to an end?
Answer on page 22.

15. There have been 12 major-league players who hit two grand slams in the same game. Four of them were Red Sox players. How many of the four can you name?
Answer on page 22.

16. What is the largest number of home runs Red Sox batters banged out in a single game?
Answer on page 22.

17. Four Red Sox batters, in succession, homered against the Yankees. When was it? Who were they?
Answer on page 22.

18. One Red Sox batter once hit two three-run homers in the same inning. Who was it?
Answer on page 22.

19. A Red Sox ballplayer went to Camden Yards not all that long ago, and hit five home runs over the course of back-to-back games. Who was it?
Answer on page 23.

20. "Put me in, coach!" Which Red Sox player became the first to hit a pinch-hit home run in both games of a doubleheader?
Answer on page 23.

21. Who holds the record, though, for the most pinch-hit homers in a single season?
Answer on page 23.

22. Who holds the team record for the most homers hit on Opening Day?
Answer on page 23.

23. Which Red Sox player hit home runs off a father and, years later, the father's son?
Answer on page 23.

24. Which Red Sox player had a year in which he hit 10 more homers than the number of times he struck out?
Answer on page 23.

25. Ted Williams hit 521 home runs. How many were game-winning homers?
Answer on page 23.

26. How many inside-the-park home runs did Ted Williams hit?
Answer on page 23.

27. In 1973, the American League instituted the designated hitter. Who was the first major-league DH to hit a homer?
Answer on page 24.

28. In 1960, Ted Williams famously homered in his last major-league at-bat. Which other Boston batter did it just two years later?
Answer on page 24.

29. There had been a batter before Ted Williams who had also homered in his last at-bat—him never appearing in another big-league game due to suicide. Who was that?
Answer on page 24.

30. Which Sox player homered in the most consecutive games?
Answer on page 24.

31. Which player has the most three-homer games in the course of his career?
Answer on page 24.

HOME RUNS

ANSWERS

1. Ted Williams—13 of them.

2. Ted Williams—17 of them.

3. Babe Ruth, who hit four grand slams in 1919. May 20—as a pitcher; June 30, as a first baseman; July 12, as a left fielder; and July 18, also as a left fielder.

4. In 1915, he hit four. In 1916, he hit only three—tied for the lead with Del Gainer and Tillie Walker.

5. Bill Mueller, on July 29, 2003. Unsurprisingly, Boston won that game, 14–7, in Texas against the Rangers.

6. David Ortiz hit 54 home runs in 2006. His 137 RBIs also led the league that year, as did his 119 walks, and 355 total bases.

7. In 1938, Jimmie Foxx had 10 multi-homer games.

8. There were three losses in there, despite Foxx doing his part to win. Three times his second homer was the game-winner. The one on August 23 was a walk-off grand slam for a 14–12 win over the Indians.

9. Way more than 10—they have hit 23 walk-off grand slams. The first was the one hit by Foxx on August 23, 1938. Some of the names are not ones well-known in team history—players like Jake Jones, Bob Zupcic, and Rico Brogna. The most recent was Pablo Reyes on August 7, 2023.

10. Creighton Gubanich in Oakland on May 3, 1999. The Red Sox scored 11 runs in the game but lost, 12–11. Daniel Nava did it, too, on June 12, 2010.

11. Jake Jones played in parts of four seasons for the Chicago White Sox. On June 14, 1947, he was traded to the Red Sox (for Rudy York). The next day he played in a doubleheader for Boston against Chicago, homering in a 7–3 first-game win, then hitting a grand slam in the bottom of the ninth for an 8–4 Red Sox victory.

12. Vern Stephens—August 13, 1949, and August 2, 1950.

13. Don Buddin, on July 11, 1959, hit off Bob Turley for an 8–4 win in the 10th inning.

14. Clyde Vollmer on July 28, 1951, hit off Bob Feller. The score was 2–2 after nine. Both teams scored once in the 15th. Starter Mickey McDermott was still pitching for Boston. He gave up another run in the top of the 16th, driven in by Larry Doby. Ted Williams doubled home Johnny Pesky to re-tie the game, but Feller walked two more and Vollmer slugged the game-ending grand slam.

15. Jim Tabor (July 4, 1939); Rudy York (July 27, 1946); Nomar Garciaparra (May 10, 1999); Bill Mueller (July 29, 2003).

16. The answer is eight. It happened on September 4, 2013. The final score was Boston 20, Detroit 4. David Ortiz hit two of them, with six other teammates joining in (Stephen Drew, Jacoby Ellsbury, Will Middlebrooks, Daniel Nava, Ryan Lavarnway, and Mike Napoli).

17. On Sunday evening, April 22, 2007, the Yankees had a 3–0 lead over the Red Sox at Fenway. With nobody on and two outs in the bottom of the third, Chase Wright served up a home-run ball to Manny Ramirez. In a span of nine more pitches, homers were hit by J. D. Drew, Mike Lowell, and Jason Varitek. A three-run homer by Lowell later in the game gave Boston a 7–5 win.

18. David Ortiz, both of them plating J. D. Drew and Dustin Pedroia each time. They were part of a 10-run first inning on August 12, 2008, against the Rangers. The Red Sox won, but only by virtue of scoring two more runs than the 17 runs the Rangers eventually put forth. All 10 Red Sox runs were off starter Scott Feldman, who stayed in the game until loading the bases in the third inning.

19. Mookie Betts, who homered three times in a 6–2 win on May 31, 2016, and then hit a homer in the first inning and another homer in the second inning the very next day. Boston lost the June 1 game, however, 13–9.

20. Joe Cronin, against the Philadelphia Athletics on June 17, 1943. He hit a three-run homer in the seventh inning of the first game, which Boston won, 5–4, and a three-run homer in the eighth inning of the second game, bringing them within one run. But the Athletics won, 8–7. Who was the "coach" who called upon Cronin? It was Cronin himself, Red Sox manager, from 1935–47.

21. It was Joe Cronin, that same year—1943. It still stands as the American League record.

22. Dwight Evans did it four times, but Carl Yastrzemski did it six times—spanning parts of three decades: 1963, 1968, 1973, 1974, and 1980. In 1968, he hit two, one of them an inside-the-park home run.

23. Ted Williams homered off White Sox pitcher Thornton Lee on September 17, 1939, and his son Don Lee of the Washington Senators, on September 2, 1960.

24. In 1941, Ted Williams homered 37 times. He struck out 27 times. It wasn't the only time: in 1950 he homered 28 times and struck out 21, in 1953 he homered 13 times and struck out 10, and in 1955 he homered 28 times and struck out 24.

25. The book *"The Kid" Blasts a Winner* (Summer Games Books, 2002, by Bill Nowlin) details 110 game-deciding home runs.

26. One. A significant one. It was mid-September, and the team had lost six games in row while trying to clinch the pennant. In the top of the first inning on September 13, 1946, he hit an IPHR off Red Embree in Cleveland—the only run of a 1–0 game, and it was the win that did clinch the pennant.

27. Orlando Cepeda. With 15 seasons under his belt and 358 career home runs, he came to the Red Sox in 1973 and in his third game—April 8, against the Yankees—hit a walk-off home run to left field in the bottom of the ninth. It was one of 20 homers he hit that season.

28. Just two years after Williams, Don Gile did the same—to very little fanfare other than for the fans that September 30, 1962, who enjoyed it producing a walk-off win. Unlike Williams, Gile was only twenty-seven and could well have made many more years in the game, but he was far from a slugger. Indeed, it was just the third home run of his career, and he had come into the day's game without even one hit all season long (despite 37 plate appearances).

29. Chick Stahl, who had played four years for Boston's National League team (1897–1900) and then six seasons for the brand-new Boston Americans. He had a 10-year career batting average of .304 with 36 home runs. He homered in his last at-bat of the year, on October 6, 1906. A month later, he married and also agreed to manage the team in 1907. Sadly, the stress of being manager that spring was too much, and he took his life by ingesting carbolic acid on March 25, 1907.

30. Rafael Devers homered on May 15, 2024, and then again on the 16th, 17th, 18th, 19th, and 20th. Oddly, the Red Sox lost the first four of those games, but then won the final two.

31. Mookie Betts did it five times—twice in 2016, twice in 2018, and once in 2019.

PITCHING

1. Who was the most recent Boston pitcher to throw a perfect game?
Answer on page 33.

2. Who was the only Red Sox pitcher to throw two no-hitters?
Answer on page 33.

3. What might one say was the most unusual thing about Howard Ehmke's no-hitter of September 7, 1923, in Philadelphia?
Answer on page 33.

4. Which Red Sox pitcher threw a no-hitter in his very first game for the Red Sox?
Answer on page 33.

5. Which Red Sox pitcher threw a no-hitter and drove in the only run needed to win the game with a home run?
Answer on page 33.

6. Which pitcher had the very best single-season earned-run average in American League history?
Answer on page 33.

7. Which pitcher had the best career ERA of any team pitcher?
Answer on page 34.

8. Which pitcher held opposing batters to the lowest batting average over the course of one full season?
Answer on page 34.

9. Two Red Sox pitchers have struck out more than 300 batters in a single season. Who were they?
Answer on page 34.

10. Which Red Sox pitcher holds the major-league record for most strikeouts in a nine-inning game?
Answer on page 34.

11. Who holds the record for major-league record for the best strikeouts-to-walks ratio (minimum career 2,000 innings)?
Answer on page 34.

12. Who is the only team pitcher to average more than 10 strikeouts per nine innings over the course of a career of at least 1,000 innings?
Answer on page 34.

13. An immaculate inning is achieved when a pitcher strikes out all three batters he faces in one inning, using the minimum nine pitches to do so. Who did it first?
Answer on page 34.

14. What a way to end a game! Which Red Sox pitcher threw an immaculate inning in the bottom of the ninth to seal a win?
Answer on page 34.

15. There have only been five Red Sox pitchers who ever threw an immaculate inning, but one of them did it three times. Who was he?
Answer on page 34.

16. It was not immaculate per the characterization, but what Red Sox pitcher threw a complete inning with only three pitches?
Answer on page 34.

17. Pitching in exactly half of one season's 162 regular-season games. Who did that?
Answer on page 35.

18. What year did the Red Sox pitching staff throw the most shutouts? Note: in all of 2018, there were *zero* Red Sox shutouts.
Answer on page 35.

19. Which pitcher threw the most shutouts in a given season?
Answer on page 35.

20. Which team pitcher holds the record for the most 1–0 shutouts in a single season?
Answer on page 35.

21. Which Red Sox pitcher had the most career shutouts?
Answer on page 35.

22. What team starter had he longest stretch of pitching without a reliever taking over?
Answer on page 35.

23. Which Sox reliever holds the team record for most saves in a season?
Answer on page 35.

24. Which Red Sox reliever has the largest number of career saves to his credit?
Answer on page 35.

25. Which team reliever has the most wins?
Answer on page 35.

26. Who had the best single-season won/loss record as a reliever?
Answer on page 35.

27. From the time he was converted to a closer in June of a given year, which pitcher gave up only two earned runs the rest of the year?
Answer on page 35.

28. Which reliever had the best overall won/loss record?
Answer on page 36.

29. When was the last time the Red Sox had two 20-game winners on the pitching staff in the same year?
Answer on page 36.

30. When was the last time the Red Sox had any pitcher win 20 games in a season?
Answer on page 36.

31. When was the last time a Red Sox pitcher won 30 games in a single year?
Answer on page 36.

32. Only four times in the twenty-first century has any Red Sox pitcher won 20 or more games. Can you name all four?
Answer on page 36.

33. Which team pitcher once threw 20 consecutive scoreless innings in one game?
Answer on page 36.

34. Who was the "losingest" pitcher of any season for Boston?
Answer on page 36.

35. Which pitcher worked in more career Red Sox games than any other?
Answer on page 36.

36. Which pitcher won the most games for the Red Sox?
Answer on page 36.

37. Which pitcher holds the team record for the most consecutive wins in a given season?
Answer on page 36.

38. Tough to ask, but which pitcher *lost* the most career games for the team? Hint: he's in the National Baseball Hall of Fame.
Answer on page 37.

39. There are three pitchers in team history who each lost more than 100 games. Who were they?
Answer on page 37.

40. Which Red Sox pitcher (with at least 20 decisions) holds the best career record against the New York Yankees?
Answer on page 37.

41. Which two Red Sox pitchers each recorded more than 2,000 strikeouts for the team?
Answer on page 37.

42. In what season did the team pitching staff post their best earned-run average, and in what season did they post their worst?
Answer on page 37.

43. Complete games are becoming rarer and rarer. When was the last time a Red Sox pitcher threw a complete game?
Answer on page 37.

44. Dropping back twenty years earlier, there was just one complete game in all of 2004. Who threw it?
Answer on page 37.

45. Harking back a bit, in what year did Boston pitchers throw the most complete games in any season?
Answer on page 37.

46. Was there ever a time a Red Sox manager left a pitcher in until after he had given up six home runs?
Answer on page 37.

47. Which Red Sox pitcher had a franchise-best 430 starts?
Answer on page 38.

48. Which team pitcher once threw almost the equivalent of three consecutive no-hitters—more than 25 consecutive innings of no-hit ball?
Answer on page 38.

49. Who was the first Red Sox pitcher to throw four consecutive shutouts?
Answer on page 38.

50. Who was the second Red Sox pitcher to throw four consecutive shutouts?
Answer on page 38.

51. Which Red Sox pitcher had a franchise-best 430 starts?
Answer on page 38.

52. Pitchers used to take their turn in the batting order, but of course they were not everyday players. When was the last time a player who played the majority of his games as a pitcher led the Red Sox in home runs?
Answer on page 38.

53. Have any Red Sox pitchers ever hit a walk-off homer?
Answer on page 38.

54. Who was the last Red Sox pitcher to hit a grand slam?
Answer on page 39.

55. Which three other Red Sox pitchers hit grand slams?
Answer on page 39.

56. Who is the only Red Sox pitcher to walk more than 1,000 opposing batters?
Answer on page 39.

57. Which team pitcher gave up the most home runs, more than twice as many as any other?
Answer on page 39.

58. This pitcher's debut saw him walk the bases loaded in the first inning—but then go to not only win the game but pitch a shutout. Who was he?
Answer on page 39.

59. While on the mound, Red Sox pitcher Ernie Shore and his Red Sox mates retired 27 consecutive Washington Senators on June 23, 1917. Not a single one ever reached base. Why was that not a perfect game?
Answer on page 39.

60. Red Sox pitcher Devern Hansack pitched a complete game against the Baltimore Orioles at Fenway Park on October 1, 2006—the last game of the season. He walked one but did not give up any hits—not one. The Red Sox won the game, 9–0. Why is Hansack not credited with a no-hitter?
Answer on page 39.

61. There was an earlier Red Sox pitcher who also pitched a complete game without giving up a hit, but is also denied no-hitter status. Who was that?
Answer on page 39.

62. Which team pitcher balked the most often in any one game?
Answer on page 40.

63. The pitching Triple Crown is to lead the league in wins, strikeouts, and ERA in the same year. Have any Red Sox pitchers ever won it?
Answer on page 40.

64. Was there ever a Red Sox pitcher who won both games of a doubleheader?
Answer on page 40.

65. He shut out the Yankees in his last game of the season—then never pitched another big-league game. Who was he?
Answer on page 40.

66. Which team pitcher holds the record for the most wins at Fenway Park in any one season, and which pitcher holds the team record for most road wins in a given season?
Answer on page 40.

67. Which twenty-first century pitcher struck out 10 or more batters in each of his first three starts with the Red Sox—something that hadn't been done for more than 100 years?
Answer on page 40.

PITCHING

ANSWERS

1. It's been a while. Cy Young (thirty-seven years old)—on May 5, 1904, against the Philadelphia Athletics. It was the first perfect game in American League history, and the only one ever thrown by a Boston pitcher.

2. Dutch Leonard, first against the visiting St. Louis Browns, on August 30, 1916 (4–0), and then on June 3, 1918, in Detroit (5–0).

3. Aside from providing a perhaps-unexpected win for a last-place team, he struck out only one batter the entire game. And then he "came within an official scorer's controversial call on what appeared to be a muffed ball of his second straight no-hitter four days later" (per Gregory H. Wolf, in Ehmke's SABR biography). The one hit in the September 11 game was by the very first batter, the Yankees' Whitey Witt.

4. Hideo Nomo—on April 4, 2001, in Baltimore. He walked three. The Red Sox won, 3–0. It was Nomo's second no-hitter; he had thrown one for the Dodgers on September 17, 1996.

5. Earl Wilson, on June 26, 1962. He held the Angels hitless at Fenway, though walked four. In the bottom of the third inning, he homered into the left-field screen off Bo Belinsky (who had thrown a no-hitter of his own in May). The Sox scored a later run and won, 2–0. Wilson was the first Black pitcher to throw a no-hitter in American League history.

6. Dutch Leonard, in 1914 had a 0.96 ERA. It was his sophomore season, age twenty-two. He was 19–5 for a team that finished in second place.

7. Smoky Joe Wood posted a career ERA of 1.99. He edged out Cy Young (2.00).

8. Opposing batters only managed to hit .167 off Pedro Martínez in the year 2000. His ERA was 1.74, leading both leagues by almost two full runs. Roger Clemens of the Yankees (ahem) was second with a 3.70 ERA.

9. First, there was Pedro Martínez, who struck out 313 in 1999. The only other is Chris Sale, who whiffed 308 in 2017.

10. Roger Clemens—and he did it twice, once home (April 29, 1986, against the Seattle Mariners) and once away, more than 10 years later (September 18, 1996, in Detroit against the Tigers). The Detroit game was his last win with the Red Sox, his 192nd—tying him with Cy Young for most team wins.

11. Pedro Martínez struck out 3,159 batters and walked 760, for a ratio of 4.1566. Let's not dwell on it, but the worst ratio (in a given year but with at least 25 games) was Ted Wingfield who walked 27 opponents in 1927 but struck out only one. He was 1–7 (5.06 ERA).

12. Pedro Martínez averaged 10.95 Ks per nine innings pitched.

13. Pedro Martínez—in the first inning of the May 18, 2002, game—the only pitcher in history to start a game that way.

14. Closer Craig Kimbrel, on May 11, 2017. The Red Sox beat the Brewers, 4–1.

15. Chris Sale—May 8, 2019; June 5, 2019; and August 26, 2021. Clay Buchholz and Rick Porcello were the other two Red Sox pitchers to throw one such inning.

16. At Anaheim Stadium, on May 11, 1969. It only took three pitches for Sonny Siebert to get three outs in the second inning—inducing a groundout (short to first), fly ball (to right field), and a foul popup (to first base). Boston beat the Angels, 7–3.

17. Mike Timlin pitched in 81 games in 2005. He had a 2.24 ERA over 80 1/3 innings pitched.

18. Exactly 100 years earlier, however, in the war-shortened 126-game 1918 season, the Sox staff threw 26 shutouts.

19. Cy Young threw 10 shutouts in 1904, and Smoky Joe Wood threw 10 shutouts in 1912. Among left-handers, the record is held by Babe Ruth, who threw nine in 1916.

20. In 1918, Bullet Joe Bush threw five 1–0 shutouts. The fourth one took 12 innings to complete, and the fifth one took 10 innings. Oddly, he also lost three 1–0 shutouts that year.

21. Cy Young and Roger Clemens, with 38 apiece. Harking back to an earlier question, Clemens's second 20-K game was a shutout, and it was his 38th.

22. Bill Dinneen worked without relief from August 19, 1903, through the rest of the season, all of 1904, and until April 25, 1905—a total of 475 2/3 innings (the equivalent of more than 52 nine-inning games) before needing relief.

23. Flash. Tom "Flash" Gordon was credited with saving 46 Red Sox games in 1998. That was exactly 50 percent of Boston's 92 wins. His ERA was 2.72 and he closed a league-leading 69 games.

24. Jonathan Papelbon (2005–11) is credited with 219 saves, well ahead of second-place Bob Stanley (132).

25. Bob Stanley leads in relief wins, with 84. Dick Radatz is second, with 49.

26. The Steamer. Bob Stanley, who went 15–2 in 1978.

27. Koji Uehara helped them win the pennant in 2013. He had already compiled 13 holds and one save. From June 26 on, he worked in 42 games and gave up just two earned runs. His season ERA was 1.09. He closed 13 postseason games, allowing just one earned run. He had one postseason win and seven saves.

28. In the games he worked in relief, Carlos Luis "Charley" Hall (1909–13) was 24–4.

29. In 2002, Derek Lowe was 21–8 and Pedro Martínez was 20–4. Back in 1946, there was 25–6 Boo Ferriss and 20–11 Tex Hughson. In 1949, there was 23–6 Ellis Kinder and 25–7 Mel Parnell. Some 53 years passed before it was done again.

30. In 2016, Rick Porcello was 22–4 with a 3.15 ERA.

31. In 1912, Smoky Joe Wood was 34–5. That's pretty good. Only two others have done it for the team . . . and they were both named Cy Young—33 in 1901 and then "only" 31 in 1902.

32. The four were Derek Lowe (21–8, 2002), Curt Schilling (21–6, 2004), Josh Beckett (21–7, 2007), and Rick Porcello (22–4, 2016).

33. Joe Harris, who lost the September 1, 1906, game, 4–1, despite all those scoreless innings—one after another from the fourth through the 23rd inning. In the 24th he faltered, and Philadelphia scored three unanswered runs. Jack Coombs went the distance for the Athletics.

34. The immortal Joe Harris. Despite a career 3.31 ERA, he was 3–30 for Boston. In 1906, he was 2–21. He lost every one of his first 14 decisions, then won a game. He won another one 10 games later, then lost his final six. And was brought back for 1907. He was 0–7 in '07.

35. Bob Stanley—"the Steamer"—worked his whole big-league career with Boston. He appeared in 637 games, 85 of them as a starter. He finished 115–97 with a 3.64 ERA.

36. Actually, there is a tie at the top of the list—192 wins for Cy Young and 192 wins for Roger Clemens. Third was Tim Wakefield, with 186.

37. Given that Joe Wood's record was 34–5 in 1912, he'd be a pretty good guess. And you'd be right—he had two stretches of eight consecutive wins that year.

38. He's also no longer with us, so his feelings can't be hurt. Red Ruffing started his career with the Red Sox in 1924 and never had a winning record. He lost 96 games against just 39 wins. He was traded to the Yankees and won 231 games for them.

39. To be allowed to lose that many games, perhaps you won a lot more. The three pitchers were Cy Young (192–112), Roger Clemens (192–111), and Tim Wakefield (186–168).

40. Babe Ruth. For the Red Sox, he was 17–5 against the Yankees, his best year was 1917 (5–0). Probably his best game was the 1–0 three-hitter on June 22, 1916.

41. Roger Clemens (2,590 Ks) and Tim Wakefield (2,046).

42. The best season was 1904, when the team as a whole had a 2.12 ERA. In the COVID-shortened season of 2020, the team ERA was 5.58. The worst ERA in a full season was 1932's 5.02.

43. It wasn't that long ago—on April 17, 2024, Tanner Houck shut out the visiting Cleveland Guardians, 3–0, allowing just three hits, walking no one and striking out nine. He threw just 94 pitches. The game lasted 1:49.

44. Pedro Martínez threw the team's only complete game of the year, a 6–0 shutout of visiting Tampa Bay. He struck out 10, walked no one, and only threw 109 pitches.

45. In 1904, the team threw 148 complete games. They only played 154 games. That means that there were just six games all year long in which a reliever was called upon. Relief stints could be lengthy. Cy Young was the reliever in three games, working a total of 19 1/3 innings!

46. There was. And the pitcher won the game! The date was August 8, in the championship season of 2004. The pitcher was Tim Wakefield. In Detroit, Wake gave up one solo homer in the first inning, back-to-back solo homers in the second, and two more homers in the third inning, giving the Tigers a 6–3 lead. And then another solo shot in the sixth. Detroit scored all nine of their runs on home runs, after Mike Timlin gave up a two-run shot in the eighth. But the Red Sox scored 11 runs, and prevailed.

47. The just-noted Tim Wakefield, over the course of 17 seasons. He won 186 games (as mentioned above), third only to Cy Young and Roger Clemens.

48. Cy Young. He did so during a span beginning in April 1904, which included seven innings of no-hit relief on the 30th, his perfect game on May 5, and the first 6 1/3 innings of his next game, on May 11. He had not allowed a hit in either of his last two innings back on April 25. It all added up. But his game wasn't over yet, after yielding the hit in the seventh inning on the 11th. He kept pitching and won that game—after 15 innings of shutout ball, 1–0.

49. Ray Culp shut out Minnesota on six hits on September 13, 1968, then shut out the Orioles on the 17th. He threw a one-hit shutout against the Yankees on the 21st, and shut out the Senators, 1–0, on the 25th. Rather than glide into the winter that way, he had one final start and lost, 4–2, but ended the season 16–6 (2.91 ERA).

50. The only other one to do it was Luis Tiant, in 1972. On August 19, he shut out the White Sox in Chicago, then came back to Fenway and shut out the Rangers on the 25th and the White Sox again on the 29th. His fourth in a row was on September 4 in Milwaukee. He finished 15–6, with a 1.91 ERA.

51. Tim Wakefield started 430 games for the Red Sox—and relieved in 130 other games.

52. You might well have guessed Babe Ruth. If you did, you're correct. In 1915, he played in 42 games, 32 of them as pitcher. His four homers were twice as many as anyone else on the team. In 1916, he played in 67 games, 42 of them as pitcher. His three homers were tied for the team lead.

53. Strangely, it's happened four times—three of them within a 12-month stretch, and all by the same pitcher. Wes Ferrell hit those three on August 22, 1934, and then in back-to-back days on July 21 and 22 in 1935. A few weeks later, Jack Wilson hit one on September 2. Ferrell had started that September 2 games, but gave up seven runs in the first two innings, so Wilson took over and threw nine innings, before hitting the homer in the bottom of the 11th.

54. It was the only home run of his Ellis Kinder's career—on August 6, 1950, in the first game of a doubleheader against the White Sox at Comiskey. It was hit off Billy Pierce, later a seven-time All-Star for Chicago. He drove in two more runs the following inning, and Boston won, 9–2.

55. Babe Ruth (May 20, 1919), Lefty Grove (July 27, 1935), and Wes Ferrell (August 12, 1936).

56. He struck out almost twice as many—Tim Wakefield, who walked 1,095 while with the Red Sox, but struck out 2,046.

57. Opponents hit 401 off Tim Wakefield. Next was Roger Clemens, with 194.

58. Dave Ferriss, on April 29, 1945, against the Athletics at Philadelphia's Shibe Park. He pitched a 2–0 shutout while going 3-for-3 at the plate.

59. It could hardly have been more perfect. The first batter walked on four pitches from Babe Ruth, who was so incensed at the plate umpire that he got ejected from the game. Shore took over. On his first pitch, the runner on first was caught stealing. Shore retired every batter he faced—the next 26, in addition to the one he had inherited. But it was not technically a perfect game.

60. The game was called due to rain after five full innings, the Sox scoring their ninth run in the bottom of the fifth. It goes in the books as a win, and as a complete game. But not as a no-hitter, due to a 1991 committee ruling that required a full nine innings to count as a "no-hitter."

61. Matt Young, in his first start of 1992, on April 12 at Cleveland Stadium. Young faced 32 batters, walking seven of them but not giving up even one hit. The Indians scored one run on an error, a later run on a fielder's choice, and led the Red Sox, 2–1, heading into the ninth. When Boston failed to score, the game was over. Opposing pitcher Charles

Nagy had surrendered nine hits, but just the one run. And Young never got to pitch the ninth inning that might have become a rule-book no-hitter.

62. John Dopson—on June 13, 1989, he balked four times, tying an American League record with four others. The major league–record is five (Bob Shaw, Milwaukee, 1963). One of Dopson's balks resulted in a run scoring, but Boston still beat Detroit, 8–7.

63. Cy Young won it in the team's first year (before they were named Red Sox), with 33 wins, 158 strikeouts, and a 1.62 ERA. It was 99 years until another team pitcher did it—Pedro Martínez in 1999 with 23 wins, 313 strikeouts, and a 2.07 ERA.

64. There was—two of them. The first was Ray Collins on September 22, 1914, in Detroit. He was 17–12 coming into the first game, allowed 12 hits, but saw Boston win, 5–3. After facing 39 batters in the first game, he took on 29 more in the second game, allowing just four hits in a game called after eight innings, and won, 5–0. The second was Carl Mays on August 30, 1918. He shut out the Athletics 12–0, in the first game and then won the second game, 4–1. He had faced 68 batters and given up 13 hits, walking two, for his 20th and 21st wins of the season.

On June 28, 1919, Mays shut out the Yankees in the first game of a doubleheader, but lost the second game, 4–1.

65. Right-hander Brian Denman, age twenty-six, improved his rookie-year record to 3–4, but recorded a 5.02 ERA in Triple A in 1983 and just never made it back to the big leagues.

66. Smoky Joe Wood won 18 home games in 1912, and he won 16 games on the road. He holds both records.

67. Rich Hill—starting a few games after a long career as a reliever—did so on September 13, 20, and 25 in 1915. Hill worked for 14 different teams over the course of his long career, including four stints with the Red Sox (2010–12, 2015, 2022, and 2024).

FIELDING

1. Which Red Sox outfielder executed the most unassisted double plays in a season?
Answer on page 43.

2. When was the last time a Red Sox player executed an unassisted triple play?
Answer on page 43.

3. Which outfielder took part in three double plays, all in the same game?
Answer on page 43.

4. Is it true that the Red Sox committed four errors in the first game of the 2004 World Series?
Answer on page 43.

5. Did an error-prone Red Sox team commit four errors in Game Two of the 2004 World Series?
Answer on page 44.

6. Has there ever been a time that a fielder committed an error in back-to-back plays during postseason play?
Answer on page 44.

7. Was there ever a time that a Red Sox fielder committed three errors in one postseason game?
Answer on page 44.

8. Which Red Sox player won the most Gold Gloves? Hint: it was not Don Buddin.
Answer on page 44.

9. Is it true that Ted Williams threw out more than 100 opponents over the course of his career?
Answer on page 44.

10. Who holds the American League record for most assists by a first baseman?
Answer on page 44.

11. More errorless games in one season?
Answer on page 44.

12. What is the longest streak of error-free games?
Answer on page 44.

13. Who was the Red Sox player who pulled off the hidden ball trick more than once against the very same team?
Answer on page 44.

14. Which catcher holds the major-league record for the most no-hitters caught?
Answer on page 45.

FIELDING

ANSWERS

1. Tris Speaker *twice* had two in a season: April 21 and August 8, 1914, and April 18 and 29, 1918. Over the course of his time in Boston, he took part in 64 double plays.

2. It was on July 8, 1994, a Friday night at Fenway against the Seattle Mariners. It was also the debut game for Álex Rodríguez. The Mariners led, 2–0, and had runners on first and second with nobody out in the top of the sixth. Both baserunners were off with the pitch. Mark Newfield lined the ball to Sox shortstop John Valentin, who then stepped on second and tagged the oncoming runner. It was the 10th such play in major-league history. Valentin was the first batter up in the bottom of the sixth and he homered, kicking off a four-run rally that won the game. When the play was executed, most of the audience, the broadcasters, and many of the players didn't realize what they had witnessed.

3. Ira Flagstead, on April 19, 1926.

4. After their dramatic comeback, winning the final games of that year's ALCS against the Yankees, the Red Sox did indeed commit four errors in Game One of the World Series against the Cardinals. Manny Ramírez committed two and both Kevin Millar and pitcher Bronson Arroyo committed one apiece. Each one of them led to a run, but Boston won, 11–9.

5. Yes, they did. The second game in a row. Including back-to-back errors in the top of the sixth. One run scored on the miscue in the fourth but none of the errors cost a run. Boston won, 6–2.

6. Indeed, it happened in the just-mentioned 2004 World Series Game One. In the top of the eighth inning, the Cardinals scored two runs to tie the score, 9–9. Both runs scored on back-to-back plays, both errors committed to left fielder Manny Ramírez. On the first one, he failed to pick up the ball cleanly. On the second, the runner scored from second base when Ramírez stumbled and let the ball glance off his glove, his spikes apparently caught in a drainage plug.

7. There was—third baseman Bill Mueller committed not just one, not just two, but three errors all in the same game—Game Two of the 2004 World Series. Only one cost a run. It was the second Series game in succession that the Sox had committed four errors. At the plate, Mueller hit .429

8. Primarily playing right field from 1976 through 1985, Dwight Evans won eight Gold Gloves. Second on the list is Carl Yastrzemski, with seven, mostly for work in left field. Fred Lynn, Dustin Pedroia, and Mookie Betts each have four with Boston. The award has been presented since 1959.

9. It is true. He threw out a lot more—he had 140 assists as an outfielder (and two more from the one time he pitched). His 12 assists in 1949 led the league.

10. Bill Buckner, with 184 in the 1985 season. He had the major-league record until Albert Pujols recorded 185 in 2009.

11. In 2016, there were 106 errorless games.

12. In 2016, the team played 18 consecutive error-free games, from September 13 through October 1 but committed an innocuous one the next day, in the final game of the regular season.

13. Marty Barrett, against the Angels on July 7, 1985, in Anaheim and then just two weeks later, to the day, on July 21 against the Angels at Fenway Park. The baserunners deceived were not novices—Doug DeCinces and Bobby Grich, both with more than 10 years of big-league experience.

14. Jason Varitek caught four official no-hitters: Hideo Nomo (April 4, 2001); Derek Lowe (April 27, 2002); Clay Buchholz (September 1, 2007); and Jon Lester (May 19, 2008). Varitek also caught the complete game thrown by Devern Hansack, on October 1, 2006—which was a win, a complete game, and in which the opposing team never got a hit—but not defined as a "no-hitter" because it didn't run nine full innings.

CHAMPIONSHIPS

1. What remarkable accomplishment did the Red Sox achieve to start each of the two centuries in which the team has played?
Answer on page 53.

2. True or false: the Red Sox won the first World Series ever played.
Answer on page 53.

3. What else did the team do, way back in 1904, that no other team has done since?
Answer on page 53.

4. In 2004, the Red Sox won their first World Series in 86 years. What particular obstacle did they overcome that year, which no other team from either league has ever done?
Answer on page 53.

5. The 2004 Red Sox became known as "The Idiots" and the 2013 Red Sox as "The Band of Bearded Brothers." What was the moniker for the 2007 Red Sox?
Answer on page 53.

6. The first World Series win of the twenty-first century famously came after an 86-year drought, in 2004. How bad had the drought been in some of the preceding years? From 1986 through 1996, how many playoff games did they lose, one after the other?
Answer on page 53.

7. What might be said to have distinguished the 2018 Red Sox from other Boston title teams?
Answer on page 54.

8. There was a Red Sox world championship team that only won 75 regular-season games. Which team was that?
Answer on page 54.

9. The 1912 World Series featured a game unlike any other postseason Red Sox game. It was the first Series game ever played at Fenway Park. In what way was it different from any other World Series game played there?
Answer on page 54.

10. In what way did the final game of the 1912 Series mirror Game Two that year?
Answer on page 54.

11. Two years later, what was unusual about every one of the home games played at Fenway Park in the 1914 World Series?
Answer on page 54.

12. The year after that, the Red Sox won the 1915 American League pennant. What was unusual about Fenway Park that postseason?
Answer on page 54.

13. The Braves played their World Series home games at Fenway Park in 1914, then the Red Sox played theirs at Braves Field in 1915. The Red Sox won the pennant again in 1916 and 1918. Where did they play those games?
Answer on page 55.

14. "The Sultan of Swat"—Babe Ruth—played for the Red Sox in the 1915 World Series. What were his stats?
Answer on page 55.

15. When the Red Sox won the final game of the 1918 World Series—the last Series they would win for 86 years, how did they score the two runs it took to beat the opposing Cubs, 2–1?
Answer on page 55.

16. What was an even longer season-ending wait for Red Sox fans than the 86 years from 1918 to 2004?
Answer on page 55.

17. Speaking of that 86-year wait, and given that life expectancy for someone born in 1900 was, more or less, 47 years (it was dramatically lower for Black Americans—just 33 years), was there anyone who actually experienced Red Sox winning in 1918 and again in 2004?
Answer on page 55.

18. The Red Sox have played in the World Series 13 times. They won nine times and lost four times. What was the common ingredient in every one of the losses?
Answer on page 55.

19. Which Red Sox manager presided over more World Series wins—Jimmy Collins, Jake Stahl, Bill Carrigan, Ed Barrow, Terry Francona, John Farrell, or Álex Cora?
Answer on page 55.

20. Three teammates on the 2007 Red Sox added another world championship ring in 2009 with the New York Yankees. Who were they?
Answer on page 55.

21. Which Red Sox player appeared in more World Series than any other?
Answer on page 55.

22. Ask 100 Red Sox fans who was the MVP of the 2018 World Series, and it is a fair bet that 90 percent of them could not come up with the right answer, even for something so recent. Who was the MVP of the 2018 World Series?
Answer on page 56.

23. That 2018 Series had a rather long Game Three. How long did it last, and who won?
Answer on page 56.

24. Who hit the first Red Sox postseason grand slam at Fenway Park?
Answer on page 56.

25. Which Red Sox pitcher once threw 29 consecutive scoreless innings in World Series games?
Answer on page 56.

26. Who was the last Red Sox pitcher to drive in runs during a World Series game?
Answer on page 56.

27. Which two team pitchers both won three of the four winning games in a single year's World Series?
Answer on page 56.

28. After 1915 and 1916, the Red Sox never finished first two years in succession in the American League standings again for more than 100 years—true or false?
Answer on page 56.

29. What Red Sox pitcher recorded not only the first out of the first game of a World Series run, but also the final out of the last game of that year's Series?
Answer on page 57.

30. Is it true that one relief pitcher closed every game of the World Series one year?
Answer on page 57.

31. After winning the 2004 World Series, the Red Sox gave a championship ring to every player on the team. Was it a colossal mistake that they gave one to someone who never appeared in a single game for the Red Sox, but actually played against them during a game in June?
Answer on page 57.

32. For their most recent world championship (2018), there were five players who worked at least one regular-season game but fewer than five. Dustin Pedroia—who already had two World Series rings—added a third, despite only appearing in three games. Can you name the other four?
Answer on page 57.

CHAMPIONSHIPS

ANSWERS

1. They went on a championship binge in the first 18 years of each new century. In the first 18 years of the twentieth century, they won the World Series five times: 1903, 1912, 1915, 1916, and 1918—never losing once. No other American League team won more than three Series during that stretch. In the first 18 years of the twenty-first century, they went on another binge, winning the World Series four times: 2004, 2007, 2013, and 2018. No other team won more than two Series during that stretch.

2. It's actually false, in that while Boston's American League team won the first World Series ever played; they were not named the Red Sox until the 1908 season.

3. They won the league pennant but had no opponent in the World Series. The NL champion New York Giants declined to play them.

4. When Milwaukee was swept in the 2025 NLCS, it represented the 41st time that the team, which was down 0–3 in a seven-game postseason series, went on to lose the series. Only once in 42 times has the team that lost the first three games come back to prevail. That time was in 2004.

5. They didn't really have one.

6. They lost 13 consecutive postseason games. Every one of them. They lost both Game Six and Game Seven of the 1986 World Series against the Mets; a win in either one would have given them the championship.

In 1988, they were swept in four ALCS games by Oakland. In 1990, like déjà-vu, they were swept in four ALCS games by Oakland. In 1995, after a Division Series had been introduced to precede the LCS, they were swept in three ALDS games by Cleveland. Finally, in 1993, they scored 11 runs in the first playoff game and won—before losing the next three and getting eliminated.

7. The team won 108 regular-season games (108–54, exactly two-thirds of the games played). Prior to 2018, the most wins a Red Sox team ever enjoyed was the 105 wins by the 1912 team. That 105–49 team had a higher regular-season winning percentage, .691.

8. The 1918 team only played a 126-game schedule. They finished 75–51. Three years later, they won 75 games again but the post–World War I schedule had reverted to 154 games and with their 79 losses in 1921 they were 23 1/2 games behind the first-place Yankees.

9. A tie game—Game Two ended in a 6–6 tie after 11 innings, the game called due to darkness. Both teams scored once in the 10th, prolonging the tie. The home team neither won nor lost. The Series went to eight games, Boston beating the Giants 4–3–1.

10. It also went to extra innings, with the Giants then taking a 2–1 lead in the top of the 10th (the run driven in by Fred Merkle) but then the Red Sox got to Christy Mathewson for two runs, driven in by Tris Speaker and Larry Gardner.

11. The Red Sox were not the home team in any of the games. The National League's Boston Braves hosted the Philadelphia Athletics, accepting an invitation to play the Boston home games at Fenway Park because of its larger capacity. The Braves swept the Series, winning Games Three and Four at Fenway.

12. It remained devoid of fans. The Red Sox played all their World Series home games down the street at the brand-new larger-capacity Braves Field, drawing more than 84,000 fans over the two home games (both of which they won, 2–1).

13. No, not in Providence or Hartford. They played 1916 again at Braves Field, but played 1918 in their true home at Fenway Park.

14. He pinch-hit in the top of the ninth in Game One, with the Red Sox down 3–1 and a runner on first base with one out. He grounded out to first base, unassisted, and then never played again, in any capacity. That was it. The Red Sox did win the next four games, and the Series.

15. Both scored on an error by Cubs right fielder Max Flack. Sox fans indeed had to wait 86 years until winning another World Series, but Cubs fans had to wait from 1908 to 2016—108 years! It's safe to assume most Red Sox fans were pulling for the Cubs in 2016. Chicago's other team—the other Sox team, the Chicago White Sox—had suffered an 88-year wait, from 1917 to 2005. With their 2005 win, it was the back-to-back breaking of Sox droughts, first Boston and then Chicago.

16. Winning the World Series at home. After doing so in 1918, the Red Sox have only once celebrated a World Series win at home—in the year 2013, some 95 years later.

17. There couldn't have been many, but there was at least one. Kathryn Gemme was born in 1894 and took in some regular-season games in 1918, as well as one in May 2004 as a guest of the Red Sox, arranged by this author. She lived to age 112 in the year 2006.

18. Each of those four Series went the full seven games: 1946, 1967, 1975, and 1986.

19. Two are tied: Bill Carrigan (1915, 1916) and Terry Francona (2004, 2007). The others each won one time.

20. Kevin Cash, Eric Hinske, and Johnny Damon—who also sported a 2004 Red Sox world champion ring.

21. There were two players who have appeared in four apiece: outfielder Harry Hooper and infielder Heinie Wagner. Both were on the championship teams in 1912, 1915, 1916, and 1918.

22. Steve Pearce. He only played in 50 games for the team during the regular season. In the Series against the Dodgers, he drew a bases-loaded walk in Game Two, tying the score. Two pitches later, the Sox took the lead for good. In Game Four, he homered to tie the score, then hit a three-run double his next time up. In the clinching Game Five, his first-inning two-run homer gave the Sox a lead they never relinquished. As a bit of a bonus, he hit another homer later in the game.

23. The game lasted 7 hours and 20 minutes at Dodger Stadium, ending at 3:30 a.m. Eastern Time. It ran 18 innings. Tied 1–1 after nine, each team scored once in the 13th—and the game went on. The Dodgers won it on a solo home run by Max Muncy, but it was the only game they won in the whole 2018 Series.

24. A nice way to kick off a must-win game, and by a player who had yet to drive in even one run in the first eight playoff games. In the bottom of the first inning of Game Six of the 2007 ALCS, J. D. Drew hit a grand slam. The Red Sox won the game, 11–2, and then won their next five games as well.

25. Babe Ruth. After Brooklyn's Hi Myers hit an inside-the-park home run in the first inning of Game Two in 1916, Ruth didn't allow another run the rest of the game—which ran 14 innings and ended in a 2–1 Boston win. In 1918, Ruth threw a nine-inning 1–0 shutout of the Cubs in Game One. In Game Four, he held the Cubs scoreless for seven innings. The Cubs scored twice in the eighth, but then saw Boston go ahead, 3–2, in the bottom of the inning and win the game.

26. Daisuke Matsuzaka drove in two runs in the sixth inning of Game Three of the 2007 World Series, bumping the score up to 5–0 in a game the Red Sox ultimately won, 10–5. Dice-K got the win.

27. Bill Dinneen won Games Two, Six, and Eight in 1903, and Smoky Joe Wood won Games One, Four, and Eight in 1912. In both years, one game ended in a tie.

28. It's true. The next time they topped the standings in successive seasons was 2016, 2017, and 2018.

29. In 2018, Chris Sale struck out the first two Dodgers he faced in Game One. As Dodger Stadium in Game Five, Sale came on in relief with the Red Sox leading Los Angeles, 5–1—and struck out the side.

30. Yes, Keith Foulke closed every game of the 2004 World Series. The Red Sox won all four games.

31. Right-handed pitcher Brandon Puffer worked in 85 major-league games, including working three innings of relief for the Padres in the June 10 game. He allowed a couple of runs, but Boston won, 9–3. The Padres later released him and he signed with Boston, brought up from Triple A for a total of one game, on September 2, but sat in the bullpen unused. He was designated for assignment the next day. But he *was* on the roster, in uniform for one full day and ready to work.

32. They were pitchers Justin Haley and Jalen Beeks, catcher Dan Butler, and Tony Renda (who pinch-ran in one game and scored, but never appeared otherwise). It was a very meaningful run, though, scoring in the bottom of the 10th on August 5 and giving the Red Sox a 5–4 win over the Yankees.

ROOKIE RECORDS

1. Which player holds the major-league rookie record for RBIs?
   Answer on page 63.

2. Which Red Sox rookie holds the team record for the most runs scored in their first season?
   Answer on page 63.

3. Which Red Sox rookie holds the major-league record for the most walks in their first season?
   Answer on page 63.

4. Which Red Sox rookie had the most extra-base hits his first year?
   Answer on page 63.

5. Which Red Sox rookie had the highest on-base percentage, highest slugging percentage?
   Answer on page 63.

6. Which Red Sox player holds the team record for the most home runs in his rookie year?
   Answer on page 63.

7. Which two rookies saw each of their first three base hits be home runs?
   Answer on page 63.

8. Which team rookie had the highest batting average on the team his first year?
Answer on page 63.

9. Which pitcher came closest to throwing a no-hitter in his very first game?
Answer on page 63.

10. Which rookie pitcher threw a shutout in his first big-league game?
Answer on page 64.

11. Which Red Sox player holds the American League record for most doubles in a rookie year?
Answer on page 64.

12. Which Red Sox rookie pitcher won the most games?
Answer on page 64.

13. Which Red Sox rookie pitcher boasted the best season ERA?
Answer on page 64.

14. Which pitcher struck out the most opponents his first year?
Answer on page 64.

15. Which rookie reliever had the most saves?
Answer on page 64.

16. Which rookie manager had the best first season?
Answer on page 64.

17. Which Red Sox rookie not only won the Rookie of the Year Award, but was also named Most Valuable Player that year and earned a Gold Glove?
Answer on page 64.

18. Who was the only Red Sox player to be unanimously voted American League Rookie of the Year?
Answer on page 64.

19. What Red Sox rookie hit the most home runs while still a teenager?
Answer on page 64.

ROOKIE RECORDS

ANSWERS

1. Ted Williams drove in 145 runs in 1939.

2. Ted Williams scored 131 runs in 1939.

3. Ted Williams drew 107 bases on balls in 1939.

4. Ted Williams had 86 extra-base hits—44 doubles, 11 triples, and 31 homers.

5. Ted Williams had a .436 OBP his first year and a .609 slugging percentage.

6. Walt Dropo—who hit 34 home runs in 1950 and led both leagues with 144 RBIs.

7. Billy Conigliaro on April 16 and 17 in 1969, and Mike Greenwell on September 25 and 26 in 1985. In Greenwell's case, that second hit boosted his average to .182.

8. Patsy Dougherty (.342) in 1902. Mr. Williams only hit .327.

9. Billy Rohr had a no-hitter going through 8 2/3 innings in his debut, at Yankee Stadium on April 14, 1967. Elston Howard singled but the next batter flew out and Boston won, 3–0. Rohr only won one more game that year, finishing 2–3 (with a 5.10 ERA).

10. Larry Pape thew a four-hit shutout at the Huntington Avenue Grounds on July 6, 1909, and beat the visiting Washington Nationals, 2–0.

11. Fred Lynn, who hit 47 doubles in 1975.

12. Dave "Boo" Ferriss, with 21 wins in 1945. His five shutouts that year also stands as a team record.

13. Dutch Leonard, with a .239 ERA in 1913.

14. In 2007, Daisuke Matsuzaka struck out 201.

15. Jonathan Papelbon, with 35 saves in 2006.

16. Álex Cora, whose first gig as manager was for the 2018 Red Sox, the team that won 108 games, and ultimately the World Series.

17. Fred Lynn, in 1975. The only player to have done it since is Ichiro Suzuki (for Seattle) in 2001.

18. Carlton Fisk in 1982; Jim Rice came within one vote in 1975. That other vote went to teammate Jim Rice.

19. Tony Conigliaro swung at the first pitch ever thrown to him at Fenway Park and homered to left. He was nineteen years old throughout the entire 1964 season and homered 24 times.

DIVERSITY

1. Who was the first foreign-born player to play for the Red Sox?
   Answer on page 69.

2. Who was the first Latino to play for the Red Sox?
   Answer on page 69.

3. What was the first foreign-born Latino to play on a world championship team for the Red Sox?
   Answer on page 69.

4. Who was the first African American ballplayer to play for the Red Sox?
   Answer on page 69.

5. Who was the next African American ballplayer to join the team?
   Answer on page 69.

6. Who had been the first African American player to sign with the Red Sox?
   Answer on page 70.

7. Who was the first African American ballplayer to appear in an American League game at Fenway Park?
   Answer on page 70.

8. Who was the first African American pitcher in the American League to throw a no-hitter?
Answer on page 70.

9. Was there in fact a former Negro League baseball player who then played with the Red Sox more than 30 years before Pumpsie Green, and then returned to Negro League play?
Answer on page 70.

10. Red Sox players have been born in various locales around the world. How many different countries have given birth to a Red Sox player?
Answer on page 70.

11. Who was the first foreign-born manager, and the first foreign-born team owner?
Answer on page 70.

12. Was Ted Williams the first Latino in the Baseball Hall of Fame?
Answer on page 70.

13. Who was the first Native American ballplayer on the Red Sox?
Answer on page 71.

14. Who was the first Jewish player on the Red Sox?
Answer on page 71.

15. Who was the first Asian to don a uniform for the team?
Answer on page 71.

16. Who was the first woman to play with a team of major leaguers at Fenway Park?
Answer on page 71.

17. Her father had been a player for the Red Sox in 1969 and 1970. Who was this woman who suited up for a professional baseball game played at Fenway Park in 1994?
Answer on page 71.

DIVERSITY

ANSWERS

1. It didn't take long. Win Kellum threw the first pitch ever thrown by a member of the team. A native of Waterford, Ontario, threw that first pitch on April 26, 1901. Unsurprisingly, he recorded the first strikeout, first complete game, and gave up the first hits and runs, but also bore the first loss—Baltimore won, 10–6. Win got his first win on May 8 in Washington.

2. Frank Arellanes, whose family came from Puebla, Mexico. He pitched for the Red Sox in the years 1908–10. The family indeed came from Puebla to California—but back in the 1700s, so Frank likely had a US lineage that predated many—if not most—of his teammates.

3. Eusebio González of Havana, Cuba, who hit .400 for the 1918 world champion Red Sox (albeit in just five at-bats).

4. Elijah "Pumpsie" Green, in 1959. The Red Sox were the last team in the major leagues to integrate, a full dozen years after Jackie Robinson. Why, in a city that was a major hub for the abolitionist movement in decades past? That's a question long debated. Jim Caple and Steve Buckley once noted that in those dozen years, "Black and Latin players won eight MVPs, nine Rookie of the Year Awards, five home run crowns, three batting titles and a Cy Young."

5. Earl Wilson, just seven days later.

6. Earl Wilson, who had signed back in 1953 but had his years in the minors interrupted by 1957–59 service in the Marine Corps. He did finally make the big leagues, as just noted, a week after Pumpsie Green.

7. Earl Wilson, against the Angels, on June 26, 1962. His third-inning homer won that 2–0 game.

8. Willard Brown of the St. Louis Browns (the team was not named after him) on July 25, 1947. The right fielder was 2-for-4 and scored a run, but the Red Sox won, 7–6. Both Bobby Doerr and Ted Williams homered.

9. There was—Ramón "Mike" Herrera, from Havana, Cuba. The Seamheads.com database shows him with a variety of teams and leagues, including Negro National League stints in 1920 and 1921. He played in 84 games for the Red Sox in 1925 and 1926, then returned to other play, including with the Eastern Colored League in 1928.

10. For these purposes, we are counting as separate entities Puerto Rico, Virgin Islands, England, Scotland, Wales, etc. The answer is: 30. The following are the ones with only one player: Aruba, Australia, Austria-Hungary, China, Denmark, Netherlands, Poland, Portugal, Saudi Arabia, Scotland, South Africa, and Wales.

11. The first foreign-born manager was Fred Lake (1908–09) from Cornwallis, Nova Scotia. The only other such Sox skipper was the man who succeeded Lake: Patsy Donovan, from County Cork, Ireland. The first foreign-born team owner was J. J. Lannin of Lac-Beauport, Québec, who owned the team from 1914–16, and saw the team win back-to-back world championships.

12. It depends on one's definition. This author makes that case in his book, notably titled *Ted Williams: First Latino in the Baseball Hall of Fame*. His mother, May Venzor, was born in El Paso about a year after her parents immigrated from Valle de Allende, Chihuahua, Mexico. If Williams is not "considered" the first, then Roberto Clemente would be the first, who was posthumously inducted in 1973.

13. Of course, it depends on one's definition. Per the criteria in the SABR book *Native American Major Leaguers*, it was Louis LeRoy, a Stockbridge-Munsee, who pitched just four innings in one 1910 game. The one with the longest tenure was Jacoby Ellsbury, the first Navajo in the majors, who helped the Red Sox win two world championships in 2007 and 2013.

14. Boston-born Sy Rosenthal, 1925–26.

15. The question is phrased as it is because he was not a player; he was third-base coach (1997–2000) Wendell Kim, born in Honolulu, of Korean and Hawaiian descent. The first Asian born outside the US was right-hander Jin Ho Cho (born in Jeonju, South Korea). His debut was July 4, 1998, allowing just one run in six innings but bearing the loss.

16. In a benefit game for ailing ballplayer Tommy McCarthy, on August 14, 1922, Lizzie Murphy played first base and batted third.

17. Gina Satriano pitched for the Colorado Silver Bullets pro team, with games at Fenway both in 1994 and 1995. She had pitched in three other major-league parks that year but spent the July 21, 1994, game in the bullpen, marveling at the experience—before returning to Los Angeles and her regular job working in the district attorney's office.

THE BALLPARK

1. Is it true that Fenway Park has been the home park of the Red Sox ever since the team started play?
Answer on page 75.

2. When Fenway Park first opened, is it correct that the first three scheduled games were all rained out?
Answer on page 75.

3. Which was the first opposing team to bat at Fenway Park?
Answer on page 75.

4. What team won the first big-league game played at Fenway?
Answer on page 75.

5. What was the unusual result of the first World Series game ever played at Fenway Park?
Answer on page 75.

6. Over the years, Fenway Park has become one of the top tourist attractions in Boston. As for attendance at games, true or false: the team once sold out more than 800 consecutive games.
Answer on page 75.

7. What is the fewest number of home runs hit by the Red Sox at Fenway Park over the course of a season?
Answer on page 76.

8. Who is the only batter to drive in more than 100 runs at Fenway Park itself over the course of a single season?
Answer on page 76.

9. Babe Ruth's major-league debut was for the Red Sox at Fenway Park. He hit 714 home runs in his career. In the six seasons he played with the Red Sox, how many did he hit at Fenway?
Answer on page 76.

10. Which Red Sox players on this list did NOT homer his first time up at Fenway Park? Tony Conigliaro, Rob Deer, John Kennedy, Lefty Lefebvre, Darnell McDonald, Lou Merloni, Daniel Nava, David Ortiz, Eddie Pellagrini, Curtis Pride, Manny Ramírez, Rip Repulski, Jim Rice, Vern Stephens, and Carl Yastrzemski.
Answer on page 76.

11. Is it true that the owner of the New York Yankees once held a mortgage on Fenway Park?
Answer on page 76.

12. What was the lowest attendance ever at a Fenway Park game (omitting the 2020 season of the COVID pandemic)?
Answer on page 76.

THE BALLPARK

ANSWERS

1. Nope, but almost. To be specific, the Red Sox started in 1908 (the first year they used that name) and Fenway opened in 1912, so there were four years—out of 125 through 2025—when they were the Red Sox but had another park (Huntington Avenue Grounds).

2. They started the season on the road, and were 4–1. April 18 was the planned opener, but heavy rain resulted in postponement with two games scheduled for the 19th, at 10:30 a.m. and 3:15 p.m. Rain and wet field conditions prevented both games from being played. Finally, on April 20, the first league game was played.

3. The Harvard University team, in a preseason exhibition game held at 3:30 p.m. on April 9, 1912. The Red Sox won the seven-inning game, a 2–0 one-hitter, before some 3,000 who braved snow flurries throughout.

4. The Red Sox! They beat the New York Highlanders (later Yankees), 7–6, in 11 innings. Tris Speaker singled in the winning run.

5. Neither team won. The Giants/Red Sox game ended in an 11-inning 6–6 tie. Both teams scored once in the 10th, but the game was called due to darkness after 11.

6. True—820 games, from May 15, 2003, through Opening Day on April 8, 2013. For the second game of the 2013 season, "only" 30,862 showed up on a rainy evening—and saw the Orioles score five runs in the top of the ninth to win, 8–5.

7. One. In 1916, the only homer hit at home was by Tillie Walker during the World Championship year of 1916, in the bottom of the seventh inning on June 20. The Red Sox lost the game to the Yankees, 4–1. The team hit just 13 on the road.

8. Jimmie Foxx in 1938. He drove in 104 at Fenway and 71 on the road.

9. Twelve. None in 1914, none in 1916, and none in 1918, and just one in 1915 and one 1917.

10. David Ortiz, Manny Ramírez, Jim Rice, and Carl Yastrzemski are the only players on the list who did not.

11. It's complicated, but tied into the sale of Babe Ruth to the Yankees. A 1919 court ruling indicated as much and it was not until Tom Yawkey took over control of the club that a settlement was worked out, in 1933.

12. Verifying attendance figures as reported by more than one newspaper, the game of October 1, 1964 drew just 306 fans. They saw the Red Sox win, 4–2, over the Angels. Given the capacity at the time of 33,368, that left the ballpark 99.99 percent empty.

NUMBERS

1. Ted Williams wore #9, Carl Yastrzemski wore #8, Joe Cronin wore #4—how many of the Red Sox uniform numbers of these great former Sox players can you name? Jimmy Collins, Harry Hooper, Babe Ruth, Tris Speaker, Cy Young.
   Answer on page 79.

2. What was the first year the Red Sox retired a uniform number and which number was it?
   Answer on page 79.

3. What numbers 0–100 have never yet been assigned to anyone?
   Answer on page 79.

4. What is the only Red Sox uniform number regularly worn by someone other than a living human being?
   Answer on page 79.

5. Why was #93 assigned to a player who never wore it in a game?
   Answer on page 79.

6. Which player had the longest tenure wearing just one number?
   Answer on page 79.

7. Which regularly assigned number has been worn by the largest number of different players?
   Answer on page 79.

8. Which number has been worn, overall, by the largest number of different players?
Answer on page 80.

9. What is another number sometimes worn by multiple players in the same game?
Answer on page 80.

10. Was there a time when one player wore two different numbers during the course of one game?
Answer on page 80.

11. Why did Roger Moret wear #23 for one game in 1975 rather than his usual #29?
Answer on page 81.

12. Who is the only Red Sox player to wear a #9 jersey in a game after Ted Williams first donned the number?
Answer on page 81.

NUMBERS

ANSWERS

1. None. All played before the team first issued uniform numbers, in 1931.

2. In 1984, the team retired #4 (Joe Cronin) and #9 (Ted Williams). In 1988, they retired Bobby Doerr's #1. Other numbers have been added to the list since then.

3. The number 0 has been assigned three times (first in 2018 to Brandon Phillips). No one has ever been assigned a three-digit number (100 or above). The numbers that have never been assigned—to a player, coach, etc.—are 69, 92, 95, 96, and 98.

4. Number 97 has been worn by the team mascot, Wally the Green Monster, since 1997.

5. On July 23, 2023, the Red Sox selected right-handed pitcher Norwith Gudiño from Triple-A Worcester and appointed him as the club's 27th man for that night's game against the New York Mets at Fenway Park. Per Major League Baseball rules, both teams were permitted to add an extra player for that game. Gudiño wore number 93, but never appeared in the game—or any other.

6. Carl Yastrzemski wore #8 for 23 seasons; Jim Rice wore #14 for 22 seasons.

7. Uniform #28 has been worn by 65 different Red Sox players. Number 19 has been worn by 56 and #23 by 55 players.

8. Number 42. It had been assigned to 22 different Red Sox players; the last to wear it regularly was Mo Vaughn. On April 22, 2007, Coco Crisp, David Ortiz, and coach DeMarlo Hale all wore #42 to honor the 60th anniversary of Jackie Robinson breaking the color barrier in Major League Baseball. Now, starting in 2009, on April 15, across all of baseball, players and coaches all wear #42 in honor of Jackie Robinson. Rounding down the number of players and coaches a bit, that means a minimum of 30 Red Sox people wear #42 each year. With 17 years—2009 through 2025—that's a total of at least 510 times that Red Sox clubbies have affixed the number 42 to a Red Sox uniform. In terms of the number of different personnel who have worn #42, someone with extra time on their hands could add up the number of the roster each April 15 and then begin to subtract those who have been with the team more than one season. We can further note that on August 28–30, 2020, the whole team also wore #42, the 75th anniversary of the August 28, 1945, date when Branch Rickey met with Robinson to discuss him joining the Brooklyn Dodgers.

9. Uniform #21 has been issued to 28 different players, but none regularly since Roger Clemens wore it from 1984–96. However, on September 15, 2021 (Roberto Clemente Day), there have been a number who each wore #21. That first year, the following Red Sox players and coaches wore #21: Álex Cora, Nathan Eovaldi, Tom Goodwin, Kiké Hernández, Jack López, Christian Vázquez, and Ramón Vázquez. This new tradition has continued through 2025.

10. Yes. On Opening Night 2020 (which did not come that year until July 24, due to the worldwide pandemic). During the third inning in Baltimore, the game featured pitcher Nathan Eovaldi (#7) throwing to catcher Christian Vázquez (#7). Eovaldi had been sweating a lot and changed jerseys between innings. Advised of his error, he resumed wearing his usual #17 in the fourth inning (and won the 13–2 game). There had been an earlier game—at Fenway on June 27, 1992, when third-base coach Don Zimmer mistakenly wore #32 for about half the game, rather than his assigned #34.

11. Thieves had broken into and robbed the Red Sox clubhouse and Moret had to make do with a different number jersey.

12. Pitcher Frank Sullivan, in Kansas City on August 28, 1955. Ted Williams also wore #9 in that same game. Sullivan said, "I had to change shirts every inning and wound up in the game in one of Ted Williams's uniforms." Boston won, 13–2, Sullivan's 16th win of the year, while Williams had four hits including his 25th homer. The 6-foot-6 Sullivan couldn't borrow just any jersey, particularly that of a pitcher such as 5-foot-9 Tommy Hurd.

MISCELLANEOUS

1. Is this true, that there was one time the Red Sox played at Fenway Park as the visiting team in a "road game"?
Answer on page 89.

2. What was the longest winning streak in team history?
Answer on page 89.

3. What was the longest winning streak of winning home games?
Answer on page 90.

4. One doesn't like to think of such things, but what was the longest losing streak?
Answer on page 90.

5. Was that year, 1906, the worst year in team history?
Answer on page 90.

6. Speaking of worst, what was the most lopsided home loss the Red Sox suffered?
Answer on page 90.

7. Without lingering too long in worsts, what was the biggest lead the Red Sox ever squandered?
Answer on page 90.

8. What is the longest game the team ever played?
Answer on page 90.

9. What is the largest crowd that ever attended a Red Sox game?
Answer on page 90.

10. Which manager presided over the most Red Sox wins?
Answer on page 90.

11. How many games has the team won?
Answer on page 90.

12. What was the most lopsided month of team play in terms of wins over losses?
Answer on page 91.

13. Speaking of lopsided, there is one Red Sox player who ranks #1 in a key offensive statistic. He also ranks second, third, fourth, fifth, sixth, seventh, eighth, and ninth in team history on this same stat. Who is he?
Answer on page 91.

14. Was there any Red Sox player who won the league's Most Valuable Player Award more than once?
Answer on page 91.

15. When Mookie Betts won the MVP in 2018, what other league awards and honors did he win?
Answer on page 91.

16. What might well have been the best trade the Red Sox ever made?
Answer on page 91.

17. Last-place losers? What was the worst stretch of Red Sox last-place finishes?
Answer on page 91.

18. What were the most runs the Red Sox ever scored in any one season?
Answer on page 91.

19. Which player has the most seasons scoring 100 or more Red Sox runs?
Answer on page 91.

20. With two outs, what are the most runs the Red Sox scored before making the third out?
Answer on page 92.

21. What were the most runs the Red Sox scored in an extra inning?
Answer on page 92.

22. Who holds the major-league record for most runs scored (six) in a given game?
Answer on page 92.

23. Which Red Sox batter once scored three runs in one inning?
Answer on page 92.

24. What was the worst start to a season the Red Sox ever had? Is it true they lost every one of their first eight games?
Answer on page 92.

25. What might be said to be the team's best Opening Day game against the rival New York Yankees?
Answer on page 92.

26. What was the highest-scoring game in team history?
Answer on page 92.

27. In the 1999 All-Star Game, played at Fenway Park, which Red Sox pitcher struck out the first four batters he faced and, then—after one reached on an error—struck out a fifth?
Answer on page 92.

28. In his rookie year, *Super Addition* hit .317 and won the Rookie of the Year Award. The very next year, he hit .326 while leading the league in base hits with 213. Who was this "super addition?"
Answer on page 93.

29. Winning the Triple Crown (leading the league in batting average, home runs, and runs batted in). Ted Williams won the American League Most Valuable Player Award twice (1942 and 1947). Is there any Red Sox player who won the Triple Crown, but did *not* win the MVP?
Answer on page 93.

30. What Boston sports figures played for three different major-league sports teams all from the same city?
Answer on page 93.

31. What Red Sox player's career saw him in the lineup as an active player in parts of four different decades?
Answer on page 93.

32. Is it true that Cy Young—while with Boston's team as a pitcher—also umpired two games?
Answer on page 93.

33. What was the single most lopsided day in team history?
Answer on page 93.

34. Is it correct there was a game that took 52 days to complete?
Answer on page 93.

35. What was the largest number of runs the Red Sox were behind in a given game, before rallying to win the game?
Answer on page 94.

36. Which Red Sox player had a pinch-hit inside-the-park homer in his first at-bat for the Red Sox?
Answer on page 94.

37. Who had the most inside-the-park homers in one season?
Answer on page 94.

38. Florida, Arizona . . . what was the one year the Red Sox held spring training the closest to Fenway Park of any?
Answer on page 94.

39. What is arguably the greatest comeback in Red Sox history?
Answer on page 94.

40. What long-standing American League umpire once threw a no-hitter for Boston?
Answer on page 94.

41. Counting exhibition games, the Red Sox have played in 42 of the 50 states of the USA. Which states do they need to get to in order to claim something no other team can claim?
Answer on page 94.

MISCELLANEOUS

ANSWERS

1. It is true. It was during the pandemic season of 2020, when teams only played a season of 60 games and no fans were admitted to any. The Toronto Blue Jays couldn't even play in Canada and played all their home games in Buffalo. There had been a racial justice protest in Buffalo on August 27 which precluded the teams from playing there, and it was agreed the game would be made up as the second game of two seven-inning games to be played at Fenway Park on September 4, with Toronto playing as the home team and batting last. The Jays won the first game, 8–7, but then lost, 3–2. (This author was at both games.)

There had been an earlier time, at least nominally, for four games from July 22–25, 1994. A section of the roof had fallen in at Seattle's Kingdome, so they played the four games scheduled there at Fenway instead. Each team won two games. The Red Sox did not bat in the ninth in the games they won.

2. The Red Sox once won 15 games in a row, beginning with a 12–5 win over the Yankees at Fenway Park on April 25, 1946. (That followed a 12–5 loss to the Yankees the day before.) A three-day road trip saw a sweep of the Athletics in Philadelphia. The next 10 victories were all at Fenway, over the Tigers, Indians, Browns, and White Sox (and included two by walk-offs. The streak wrapped up with a 5–4 win over the Yankees on May 10, when they came back to town. They had a 13-game winning streak in July 1948.

3. Starting on June 25, 1988, with a 10–3 win over the Orioles, the Red Sox won 24 consecutive games at Fenway Park, wrapping up on August 13 with a 16–4 win over the Tigers. Three of the wins were walk-off wins.

4. It was in 1906, when they lost 20 games in a row—every game in May from May 1 until they snapped the streak on the 25th. Sadly, every one of the losses was at home. They finished the season 49–105.

5. Nope. Their .316 winning percentage was better than 1925 (.309) and 1926 (.301, in part due to a 17-game losing streak).

6. In the year 2000, and at the hands of the Yankees no less, the Red Sox were losing 6–1 after seven innings, but the Evil Empire scored nine runs in the eighth and seven more in the top of the ninth, winning 22–1.

7. They led Toronto 10–0 after six full innings at Fenway. The Blue Jays scored 11 times and had a one-run lead heading into the bottom of the ninth. Boston tied it, but Toronto scored two unanswered runs in the top of the 12th and won.

8. Measured by innings, it was on September 1, 1906—24 innings in Boston. The score was 1–1 after six innings but then neither Philadelphia nor Boston scored until the Athletics put up three unanswered runs in the top of the 24th. Time of game was only 4:40. The game was the first of a planned doubleheader, but the second game was simply canceled.

9. Oddly enough, it was a spring training game—not a regular-season game and not a postseason game. The crowd was 115,300 at the Los Angeles Coliseum to see the Dodgers take on the Red Sox on March 29, 2008. The Red Sox won, 7–4.

10. Joe Cronin, with 1,068 wins (and 910 defeats). Terry Francona was 744–552 for Boston.

11. The Red Sox celebrated their 10,000th win on July 5, 2025. And kept on going.

12. In August 1950, the Red Sox won 24 games and lost six, winning 80 percent of their games that month.

13. Ted Williams's .553 on-base percentage in 1941 ranks tops. His .526 in 1957 ranks second. He was also tops of the team in 1954, 1942, 1947, 1946, 1948, 1949, and 1956.

14. Yes, there was—Ted Williams won it in both 1946 and 1949. The other MVPs were Tris Speaker (1912), Jimmie Foxx (1938), Jackie Jensen (1958), Carl Yastrzemski (1967), Fred Lynn (1975), Jim Rice (1978), Roger Clemens (1986), Mo Vaughn (1995), Dustin Pedroia (2008), and Mookie Betts (2018).

15. The American League batting title, a Silver Slugger, a Gold Glove, and the team won the World Series.

16. On July 31, 1997, the Red Sox traded closer Heathcliff Slocumb to Seattle. At the time he was 0–5 with a 5.79 ERA. In return, they landed Derek Lowe and Jason Varitek. Slocumb lost four games for the Mariners, ending the season 0–9. Lowe pitched in 384 games for the Red Sox and in 2004 was the winning pitcher in the final game of each of the three rounds of the postseason. Varitek became "the captain," playing in 15 seasons for Boston, driving in 757 runs, and helping earn two World Series wins.

17. It was a long time ago. Back when there were eight teams in the league and thus no divisions, the Red Sox finished in eighth place every year from 1925–30, six years in succession. From 1922 through 1932, they finished last nine times.

18. In 1950, even though they only finished third, they scored 1,027 runs. The closest they have come since then—despite the numbers of games played annually having increased—was in 2003, when they scored 961 runs. The team ERA in 1950 was 4.88. There are only six seasons in which they have recorded a worse ERA.

19. David Ortiz scored 100 or more runs 10 times. That was once more than Ted Williams.

20. On August 21, 1986, they just wouldn't quit. In Cleveland, they had a 7–1 lead in the top of the sixth with runners on first and third and two outs. There followed walk, walk, Tony Armas grand slam, walk, single, walk, double, single, walk, single, single—11 runs scored, the Indians on their fourth pitcher of the inning, and Armas coming to bat. He flied out to center.

21. The White Sox won the first game on July 8, 1973. In the second, it was 2–2 after nine. The Red Sox scored nine runs in the top of the 10th, the biggest hit a Bob Montgomery grand slam. The White Sox went down 1-2-3.

22. Two Red Sox players share the major-league record: Johnny Pesky (May 8, 1946, when the Red Sox beat the White Sox, 14–10) and Spike Owen (August 21, 1986, when Boston beat Cleveland, 24–6).

23. Sammy White did it on June 18, 1953. The Red Sox led the Tigers, 5–2 after six innings at Fenway, then scored 17 runs in the bottom of the seventh. White singled, then walked, then singled again—and scored each time.

24. Yes, sad but true. There was a war going on. In 1945, they lost every one of their first eight games. They rebounded, winning five in a row, but finished the season in seventh place.

25. April 6, 1973—the first game the two teams played after New York eliminated Boston in the final game of 1972. The Yankees kicked off the game with a 3–0 lead in the first inning, but ultimately went down to defeat, 15–5. Luis Tiant got the win; catcher Carlton Fisk had six RBIs.

26. There were 36 runs scored at Fenway Park on August 12, 2008. The Texas Rangers scored 17 runs and might have been expected to win, but the Red Sox scored 19. And they'd scored 10 of those runs in the first inning—on only seven base hits (there were two walks, and one batter reached on an error). All 10 runs off starter Scott Feldman.

27. Pedro Martínez. He tied an AL record.

28. The letters are an anagram for Dustin Pedroia. Thanks to author Chris Bradshaw for that one.

29. Yes, Ted Williams—in 1942 and 1947. Joe Gordon of the Yankees won it in 1942. He led the league in just two categories—striking out and grounding into double plays. Joe DiMaggio won it in 1947, leading in no offensive stats.

30. Pitcher Gene Conley played for the Boston Braves in 1952, the Boston Celtics in 1959–61, and the Boston Red Sox in 1961–63.

31. Ted Williams played from 1939 through the 1960 season.

32. Cy Young was 28–9 for the 1903 Boston Americans and pitched in 40 games. He was the plate umpire in the July 4 morning game in Boston, a 4–1 win over visiting St. Louis, and again on July 8, a 6–1 win over the White Sox. Umpire Jimmy Hassett had arrived late for the July 4 game, so Young filled in by mutual consent. No umpire turned up for the July 8 game, so Young from Boston and Patsy Flaherty of the White Sox shared duties. Flaherty worked three other games in later years.

33. June 23, 1931. The Sox played two against the Cleveland Indians, and lost 13–0, and then 10–0. The number of traumatized fans was limited, because the games were played in Cleveland. They were out-hit, 31–6.

34. On June 13, 1968, the Red Sox and Angels were tied 1–1 when the game was suspended so the Angels could catch a scheduled airplane flight home to California. It resumed on August 4. It was still 1–1 going into the bottom of the ninth, with Bill Harrelson pitching for the Angels. He hadn't allowed a hit in three full innings he had worked, but in the bottom of the ninth allowed a leadoff single and then walked the next two batters. In the on-deck circle was . . . Ken Harrelson (no relation). Manager Bill Rigney brought in Andy Messersmith, who gave up a walk-off grand slam. Though he had hit 26 previous home runs, this is registered as his 10th of the year since all the others had been hit during the intervening games.

35. At Fenway Park on August 28, 1950, the Cleveland Indians held a 12–1 lead after batting the top of the fourth. The Red Sox scored eight runs in the bottom of the fourth to pull closer and added six more runs later on, overcoming the 11-run deficit and winning, 15–14.

36. John Kennedy on July 5, 1970.

37. Hobe Ferris hit nine of them in 1903. The team as a whole hit 38 IPHRs that year.

38. In 1943, during World War II, they held spring training eight miles from Fenway, at Tufts University in Medford, Massachusetts.

39. Leaving aside the 2004 ALCS, the biggest comeback in one game was June 18, 1961. The Washington Senators were at Fenway Park for a doubleheader. They were leading 12–5 after the top of the ninth. The Red Sox scored eight runs in the bottom of the ninth, and won. The day's second game saw a 5–5 tie through nine, and then a second walk-off in the 13th, on a Jim Pagliaroni home run. It was Pagliaroni's grand slam that had tied the first game in the ninth, before they pushed across the 13th run.

40. Bill Dinneen umpired thirty years in the American League, beginning in 1907 through 1937 and worked in eight World Series. He is the only person to both throw a shutout in a World Series (both Game Two and the final game of the 1903 World Series were shutouts) and umpire World Series games (including the one the Red Sox won in 1916). His no-hitter was September 27, 1905, against the White Sox.

41. The states they need to get to are: Alaska, Hawaii, Idaho, Montana, North Dakota, Oregon, South Dakota, and Wyoming.

MUSIC

1. What is arguably the favorite song of most Red Sox fans?
   Answer on page 97.

2. There is another song—enjoyed both by most Sox fans and visiting partisans of other teams. This song is played at every home game. What is it?
   Answer on page 97.

3. Two other songs are also played at every Fenway Park game. Can you name them?
   Answer on page 97.

4. Fenway Park features a live organist. Who are its two longest-tenured ballpark organists?
   Answer on page 97.

5. There was a song credited by the opposing Pittsburgh Pirates as helping the Red Sox win the first World Series ever played, back in 1903. What was it?
   Answer on page 98.

6. Why do some Red Sox fans sour a bit when "Sweet Caroline" is played late in Boston home games?
   Answer on page 98.

7. Is it true that the Red Sox usually played "The Star-Spangled Banner" for more than 10 years before it became the National Anthem?
Answer on page 98.

8. After every Red Sox home win, there are two songs that follow "Dirty Water." What are they?
Answer on page 98.

9. What Red Sox player was also a fairly successful and verifiable hit, earning him a recording contract and $25,000 advance from RCA Victor?
Answer on page 98.

10. What was the first known musical group comprised of Red Sox players?
Answer on page 98.

11. Three Red Sox players sing in the chorus to the 2004 recording of "Tessie"—which debuted at Fenway on July 24, 2004. Can you name them?
Answer on page 99.

12. Those three plus a raft of others once all recorded on an album by noted Boston-area sportswriter Peter Gammons. True or false?
Answer on page 99.

MUSIC

ANSWERS

1. "(Love That) Dirty Water" by The Standells—for more than 20 years, it has been the Red Sox victory anthem, played at Fenway Park after each Red Sox home win.

2. "Sweet Caroline"—the Neil Diamond song which was a hit in 1969 and is played in the middle of the eighth inning. It was first played on a fairly regular basis on April 10, 1998, but (perhaps auspiciously) as of the beginning of the 2004 season has been played at every game.

3. "The Star-Spangled Banner" is played before every game, and "Take Me Out to the Ball Game" is played during the seventh-inning stretch.

4. They both share the same initials. John Kiley played the ballpark organ on most days from 1953–89, a stretch of some 36 years. He released an album *Red Sox Organ Music*, which featured Sox shortstop Rico Petrocelli on drums. After some other organists filled in (including another "JK"—Jim Kilroy), Josh Kantor took over on Opening Day 2003—and through the 2025 season has not missed even one game. Even during the pandemic season of 2020, Josh played the organ live at Fenway (despite there being zero fans admitted to the park, and even the broadcasters calling the games from a studio elsewhere in Greater Boston). Counting postseason games, and even one "road game" played at Fenway during that unusual 2020 season, Josh Kantor has played 1,779 consecutive games.

5. The song was "Tessie." It was a popular song of the day. The precursor to today's BoSox Club—the Royal Rooters—entrained to Pittsburgh for the away games and hired a local band. They wrote new lyrics to "Tessie" needling the opposing Pirates. Leach told Lawrence Ritter in *The Glory of Their Times*: "I think those Boston fans actually won that Series for the Red Sox. We beat them three out of the first four games, and then they started singing that damn Tessie song. . . . In the fifth game of the Series the Royal Rooters started singing Tessie for no particular reason at all, and the Red Sox won. They must have figured it was a good-luck charm, because from then on you could hardly play ball they were singing Tessie so damn loud."

6. The Red Sox could be getting wiped out, being crushed—say, 14–2 in an important game—and the mood suddenly shifts within thousands begin joyously singing the song. For fans who value winning more than momentary pleasure, well . . .

7. That is true. The song was first played (by a live band) before the game of September 9, 1918 (Game Four of that year's World Series). It had been played from time to time, going back to at least 1903 (at the team's Huntington Avenue Grounds), but became a regular feature starting with that Game Four in 1918. Boston pitcher Babe Ruth won that game, 3–2. Boston's first two runs came on a triple by Ruth. It was only on March 3, 1931, that the song was designated the National Anthem of the United States of America.

8. The victory trilogy is: "Dirty Water" by The Standells, "Tessie," the 2004 rendition by the Dropkick Murphys, and "Joy to the World" by Three Dog Night. The Fenway Park organist then plays upbeat music as the remaining fans file out of Fenway.

9. Tony Conigliaro, whose single "Limited Man" went to #1 on Worcester station WORC. His signing to RCA was depicted in the March 13, 1965, issue of music industry trade journal *Cashbox*.

10. The group was formed in 1911—the Red Sox Quartet—a barbershop-style quartet featuring Hugh Bradley and Marty McBride (tenors),

Tom O'Brien (baritone), and Larry Gardner (bass). After the season, they were booked into a number of shows on the Keith's vaudeville circuit.

11. They were Bronson Arroyo, Lenny DiNardo, and Johnny Damon. The game itself featured the oft-seen confrontation wherein Boston's Jason Varitek pushed his catcher's mitt into the face of New York Yankee Álex Rodríguez, and ended with a bottom-of-the-ninth three-run walk-off home run by Bill Mueller.

12. True. The album *Never Slow Down, Never Grow Old* (Rounder 9070) was released in July 2006. Among those who appear on the album are: Jonathan Papelbon, Kevin Youkilis, Trot Nixon, Lenny DiNardo, Tim Wakefield, Bronson Arroyo, NESN broadcaster Don Orsillo, and Red Sox GM Theo Epstein with some lead guitar. Also appearing are Juliana Hatfield, George Thorogood, Paul Barrere of Little Feat, and Kay Hanley.